ARABIC PROVERBS

Compiled & Translated by
Joseph Hankí

D1520429

HIPPOCRENE BOOKS
New York

For information, address:
HIPPOCRENE BOOKS, Inc.
171 Madison Avenue
New York, NY 10016

Cataloging-in-Publication data available from the Library of Congress.

ISBN 0-7818-0631-3

Printed in the United States of America.

ARABIC
PROVERBS

INTRODUCTION

« To understand a proverb and the interpretation;
the words of the wise and their dark sayings » is a
task that Mr. Joseph Hanki has endeavoured to make
an easy one for others. It is hoped that his labours
may be so far successful as « to give subtlety to the
simple, to the young man knowledge and discretion. »
For proverbs are the fossil records of the teachings
of the accumulated experience of past generations
preserved in a form that out–lives the experience that
formed them. By their universal applicability to all
times, since man became a « homo sapiens », the
wisdom they embody is attested.

In this collection many old acquaintances are re-
cognised as being older than our acquaintance with
them, and no doubt the origin of many proverbs,
commonly used in the West, is to be traced to the
East. We find for example among these Arabic proverbs such familiar friends as the following :

« A soft answer turneth away wrath », one of the
Proverbs of Solomon.

« He who digs a pit for his brother will fall into
it himself », also Biblical.

p. 39

p. 55

« Necessity is the mother of Invention ».

« Silence gives consent ».

« If speech is silver, silence is golden ».

and

« You cannot make a silk purse out of a sow's ear ».

Those Egyptian official gentlemen, with whom I have had friendly intercourse, I have found to have a great appreciation for proverbs and epigrams. This I remarked almost immediately after I came to their country, for I soon found it necessary to draw attention to the axiom that one man cannot serve two masters. I did not use that expression, but, instead of doing so, I remarked (through my interpreter) that there was only one captain's berth provided in a ship. To which the gentleman, whom I was trying to impress, replied with his own Arab version, (which will be found in the following collection), « With two pilots in the boat, it will sink ». I knew then that I was at least understood, even if I had not carried my point. Whether, in this particular instance, the use of proverbs was welcome, I cannot say ; but I learnt afterwards that, disassociated from any inconvenient application, the use of proverbs in conversation seemed to give pleasure.

How and when proverbs became stereotyped into their permanent forms is no easy matter to discover. From « internal evidence » they might be of any age.

« Birds of a feather flock together » may have been true of the Garden of Eden, if more than one species had been evolved before the garden was closed to the public. « Those who live in glass houses should not throw stones » might be supposed to be of less respectable antiquity than the Crystal Palace, were the same proverb not to be found in this collection. There are no accepted proverbs which seem to have been born in our time or at all recently. Were there such proverbs for instance as « That which is fittest has most survivors, « Light wires carry weighty words », or « The best machines make least noise », or « If wheels with a horse be beyond your means, be content with wheels without one », we could recognise them as contemporaries. But there are none « on the list » which bear witness in themselves of so recent an origin. We must therefore assume them all to come down to us from our distant ancestors and venerate them accordingly.

Mr Hanki has with considerable patience and trouble made a collection of the proverbs that are current in Egypt, has translated them and sought out their nearest Western relations. He has further explained the meaning and application of each for, let us hope, the enlightenment of those to whom they are « dark sayings », and for « the wise man to hear and increase learning ».

R. H. BROWN

A SELECTION

OF

MODERN EGYPTIAN PROVERBS

———∞◇◇∞———

مِد رجليك على قَدْ بساطك

Stretch your legs to the extent of your carpet
(sleeping rug).

« *Cut your garment according to your cloth* ».

———

قالوا للديك صيح قال كل شيء في اوانه مليح

They told the cock to crow. He replied : everything in its time is good.

Meaning that there is a time for everything.

———

كل واحد له قادح ومادح

Every one has a detractor and an adulator.

———

جا الخروف يعلّم ابوه الرعي

The lamb came to teach its father how to graze.

« *Teach your grandmother to suck eggs* ».

ان كان صاحبك عسل ما تلحسوش كله

If your friend is honey, do not lick him all up.

Meaning that generosity should not be abused.

السلفه تربّي العداوة

Lending engenders enmity.

كثر التنخيس يعلّم الحمير التقميص

Much goading will teach donkeys to rear.

« *Oppression causeth rebellion* ».

اللي يمدّ رجليه ما يمدّش ايديه

He who stretches his legs must not hold out his hand.

Applied to a needy man who gives himself airs.

الخضوع عند الحاجه رجوليه

Humility in asking a favor is manly.

العاقل من غمزَه والجاهل من رفصَه

The wise with a wink, and the ignorant with a kick.

« *A word to the wise* ».

كل خرابه ولنا فيها عفريت

In every ruin we find a devil.

Meaning that, wherever we go, there is always some one to thwart our plans.

———

اللي مالوش خدام يخدّم على روحه

He who has no servant must wait upon himself.

———

الخبر الشؤم يوصل بالعجل

Bad news arrives quickly.

« *Ill news travels apace* ».

———

العصفور يتفلّى والصياد يتقلّى

The bird is pluming itself and the hunter is burning with impatience.

Applied to a man who listens with equanimity to a demand urged with the greatest warmth.

———

كل رفيق يصح أخير من أخ

A congenial companion is better than a brother.

المقروص من التعبان يخاف من طرف الحبل

He who is bitten by a snake is afraid of an end of rope.

« *The burnt child dreads the fire* ».

———

اللي يشبع بعد جوعه ادعوا له بثبات العقل

To him who is replete after starvation, pray God to give firmness of mind.

Meaning that a state of affluence after poverty is liable to turn the head.

———

عداوة العاقل ولا صحبة الجاهل

Rather the enmity of the wise than the friendship of the ignorant.

———

ما ينوب المخلّص الا تقطيع الهدوم

The peace-maker does not gain except by the tearing of his garments.

« *Those who in quarrels interpose*
Must oft expect a bloody nose ».

———

من فاتك فوته

Who shuns you, shun him.

الفواجر دموعها حواضر

The impudent have their tears always ready.

Applied to one who, being reproached for misconduct, takes shelter in tears, but more generally said by a man to his wife.

———

ايش تعمل الماشطة في الوش العكِر

What can the tire-woman make out of a plain face.

« A crow is never the whiter for washing itself often ».

———

زي غيط الكرنب كله روس

Like a field of cabbages, all heads.

Said of a company everyone of which claims to be the head.

———

حب وواري واكره وداري

Love and show, hate and hide.

———

ايش ياخذ الريح من البلاط

What can the wind take from the stone-paving.

« Where there is nothing, the king loses his rights »

قبل ما ينبني الجامع اترصّت العميان

Before the mosque is built, the blind have ranged in a row.

It is the custom in Egypt to distribute alms to the poor, many of whom are blind, on the completion of a mosque and sometimes of a house. The proverb is applied to those who seek their share of the profit on a transaction before it is completed.

اتمسكن لما نتمكن

Make yourself obsequious till you gain your end.

انا كبير وانت كبير مين يسوق الحمير

I a grandee and you a grandee, who will drive the donkeys?

« *There is no accord where everyman would be a lord* ».

جا يتاجر في الحنّة كثرت الاحزان

He commenced to trade in « Hennah », and mournings became numerous.

Said of an unlucky man, « Hennah » being used at times of rejoicings to dye the fingers, toes and nails, to which it imparts a deep orange colour : the dye is produced from the leaves of the « Hennah » tree or Egyptian privet.

الامارة حلوة الرضاع مرة الفطام

Power is sweet to nurse, bitter to wean.

دبور زن على حجر مسن

A wasp buzzes on a grind-stone.

« *You cannot get blood out of a stone* ».

زي اللي بينفخ في قربه مخروقه

Like him who blows into a leaky waterskin.

Said of one engaged in a hopeless task.

المساواة في الظلم عدل

Equality in injustice is justice.

ان رأيت بلد تعبد عجل حش واطعمه

If you see a town worshipping a calf, mow grass
and feed him.

« *When at Rome, do as Rome does* ».

الشاطره تغزل برجل حمار

The clever girl spins with the leg of a donkey.

« *A good workman does not quarrel with his
tools* ».

الحجامة بالفاس ولا الحاجة للناس

Better be cupped with an axe than ask a favor from others.

Intended to convey the idea that torture, such as would be caused by substituting a blunt instrument for a lancet or razor, is the less painful of the two alternatives offered.

———

ظن العاقل ولا يقين الجاهل

The conjecture of the wise, rather than the certitude of the ignorant.

———

باب النجار تلّي مخلع

The carpenter's door is always badly hung.

« *The cobbler's wife is always the worst shod* ».

———

عادي امير ولا تعادي غفير

Make an enemy of a governor, but not of the watchman.

Meaning that a man in humble life may be of more service to you than one in a high position.

———

الحيا في الرجال يرث الفقر

Bashfulness in men engenders poverty.

اللي تحبل على الفرن تولد في الجرن

She who conceives on the oven will give birth in the « Gorn ».

The Egyptian peasantry sleep, in winter, on the oven which occupies one end of a room of every peasant's hut; the « Gorn » is an open space generally in the middle of a village where the corn is threshed and the market held. The proverb is used to signify that what has taken place secretly will eventually become known.

الشاهد يرى ما لا يرى الغائب

The eye-witness sees what the absent does not see.

الغايب حجته معه

The absent has his excuses.

« *The absent party is not so faulty* ».

زي اولاد الكلبة الابيض فيهم نجس

Like the pups of the bitch, even the white one is impure.

Said of a family or a community of such bad renown, that, even though one member be not corrupt, it will not be credited.

كثر الضحك يذهب الهيبة

Much laughter dispels gravity.

سلم من الموت اتجنن

He escapes death and goes mad.

« *Out of the frying pan into the fire* »

لما تحضر الملايكة تذهب الشياطين

When the angels arrive, the devils abscond.

Said facetiously by a guest who, on arriving, sees another leaving.

غرامة بيّنه ولا ربح بطىٔ

An evident loss rather than a distant profit.

التكرار يعلّم الحمار

Repetition will teach the donkey.

« *Practice makes perfect* »

زي ابن الرئيس ثقل على المركب وفنا على الخبزه

Like the son of the captain : a burden on the boat and a drain on the food.

Said of one who is not only useless, but an encumbrance at the same time.

الصاحب اللّي يخسر هو العدّو المبين

The friend who causes you to lose is a true enemy.

———

بيضة اليوم ولا فرخة بكره

The egg of to-day and not the hen of to-morrow.

« *A bird in the hand is worth two in the bush* »

———

طلع من المولد بلا حمص

He left the Fair without parched peas.

It is a custom to take parched peas from a Fair in Egypt, as ginger bread is taken from a country Fair in England.

Said of one who has been baulked in an enterprise and returns empty-handed.

———

اللي نقول عليه موسى يطلع فرعون

He whom we call Moses turns out to be Pharoah.

Meaning he whom we supposed to be a good man turned out to be a villain. « Ibn Faraon », son of Pharoah, or « Gins Faraon », of the nature of Pharoah, is used as term of reproach.

اللي نرضى بقليله عاش

He who is contented with his lot will live long.

القفه اللي لها ودنين يشيلوها اثنين

The basket that has two handles can be carried by two.

الحرامي الشاطر مايسرقش من حارته

The clever thief does not steal from his own street.

كشكار دايم ولا علامه مقطوعه

Bran constantly rather than fine flour seldom.

« *Better be meals many than one too merry* ».

ما حد يجي من الغرب يسر القلب

No one comes from the west and gladdens the heart.

Formerly applied to merchants from the African Ports of the Mediterranean and especially to those from Morocco who, by greater cunning and rapacity, got the better of the Arab trader.

زي حمام بلا ميّه

Like a Turkish bath without water.

Said of an assembly in a state of turmoil.

———

الجواب للسفيه السكوت عنه

The answer to insolence is silence.

———

لما تقع البقره تكثر السكاكين

When the cow falls down, knives are plentiful.

« *When a man is going downhill, everybody gives him a kick* ».

———

خادم يسرق ولا شريك يحاسب

A servant who steals rather than a partner who exacts accounts.

———

اربط البغل جنب الحمار يا يتعلم شهيقه يا نهيقه

Tether the mule near the donkey : he will learn either to « Hee » or to « Haw ».

« *He that lives with wolves will learn to howl* »

زي جمعية الاغربه اولها قاق واخرها قاق

Like an assembly of crows ; it begins with a
« Caw » and ends with a « Caw ».

Said derisively of a meeting dispersing without arriving
at any conclusion.

كلام الليل مدهون بزبده يطلع عليه النهار يسيح

The words of the night are coated with butter ;
as soon as the day shines upon them, they melt
away.

« *Words spoken in the evening the wind car-
rieth away* ».

ايش حالك اليوم قال حال الـكلاب على الكوم

How do you feel to-day ? Like a dog on a mound.

The pariah dogs becoming sick and incapable of defend-
ing themselves seek shelter on the mounds of rubbish outside
the town. Used to express a dismal condition.

من ساواك بنفسه ما ظلمك

He, who treats you as himself, does you no injustice.

ان كان الكلام من فضه السكوت من ذهب

If speech is silver, silence is golden.

———

لما تخانق الحرامية يبان المسروق

When thieves quarrel, the stolen things are visible.

« *When rogues fall out, honest men come by their own* ».

———

في الوش مرايه وفي القفا سلايه

To the face he is a mirror, and in the neck a thorn.
Said of a back-biter.

———

الحاجه ام الاختراع

Necessity is the mother of invention.

———

صباح القرود ولا صباح الاجرود

The morning of the monkeys and not of the beardless.

Meaning that it is preferable to meet a monkey the first thing in the morning, rather than to meet a beardless man. For in Egypt it is considered unfortunate by most natives, if, upon leaving the house in the morning, the first person met should be ugly, one-eyed or beardless. When this happens many will return and start again.

The monkey is regarded as the spirit of ugliness and the beardless as the spirit of evil.

العتّال ما يتفكرش ربنا الاّ تحت ·الحمل

The porter thinks not of God, save when under the weight of his burden.

فاتت عجينها في الماجور وراحت تضرب على الطنبور

She left her dough in the dough-pan and went to play on the mandoline.

« *The more women look in their glasses, the less they look to their houses* ».

وشّه يقطع الخميره من البيت

His face cuts off the yeast from the house.

Nearly every family in Egypt makes its own bread; therefore yeast is a necessity and the lack of it would be a calamity. The proverb is quoted in speaking of a man of forbidding appearance.

العداوه في الاهل والحسد في الجيران

Enmity is found in relatives and envy in neighbours.

فقر بلا دين هو الغنى التام

Poverty without debt is real wealth.

« *He, that gets out of debt, grows rich.* »

البلد اللي ما يعرفكش فيها امشي وهزّ كمك فيها

In a town where you are not known, you may walk and swing your sleeves.

The sleeves of an Egyptian townsman's garment usually extend some inches beyond the hand, and being swung they give the wearer a swaggering appearance.

———

كدب مساوي ولا صدق معفّش

A smooth lie is better than a distorted truth.

———

حبيبك يمضغ لك الزلط وعدوك يعدّ لك الغلط

Your friend chews gravel for you and your enemy counts your faults.

« *When love fails we espy all faults.* »

———

خُذ من الزرايب ولا تاخذ من القرايب

Marry from the sheepfold and not from your relatives.

Quoted to a man about to marry a relative.

———

اللّي يفتن لك يفتن عليك

He who chatters to you will chatter of you.

ابو جعران في يته سلطان

The beetle in its hole is a sultan.

« *Every cock is a king on his own dunghill.* »

ان عشقت اعشق قمر وان سرقت اسرق جمل

If you love, love a moon, and if you steal, steal a camel.

Do nothing by halves. In the East, a beautiful girl is compared to the moon and a camel is a most valuable animal.

اللّي يحب شيء يكثر ذكره

He who likes a thing will mention it often.

اللي ما يجعلنيش كحل في عينه ما اجعلوش صرمه في رجلي

He who does not make me as « *Kohl* » in his eye. I would not wear as a slipper.

Kohl is a black powder commonly composed of the smoke-black which is produced by burning a kind of « *Liban* », an aromatic resin. It is used for blackening the edge of the eyelids and eye-brows of the Egyptian women, as adornment. The expression used figuratively means that if a neighbour does not pay the speaker attention the latter will treat the former with contempt, a slipper being frequently employed as a term of reproach. In the streets of Cairo, « you, son of an old slipper » is constantly heard.

رئيسين في المركب تغرق

Twó pilots in the boat it will sink
« *Too many cooks spoil the broth.* »

البطن ما تجيبشي عدو

The womb does not bring forth an enemy.

احضر اردبك يزيد

Be present at the measuring of your corn and it
will increase.
« *The master's eye makes the horse fat.* »

زي عجايز الفرح ياكلوا ويتنَقَّروا

Like the old women at a wedding, they eat and
mock.

Rebuking discontent. Applied to one who, though perhaps
gratified even beyond his expectations, affects to despise what
has been bestowed upon him.

اللي يحت لاخيه قره يقع فيها

He who digs a pit for his brother will fall into
it himself.

عند البطون تضيع العقول

When the stomachs are concerned, wits are missing.

« *An empty belly hears nobody.* »

———

قالوا الجمل طلع المدنه قال آدي الجمل وآدي المدنه

They said : A camel ascended a minaret. He said : Here is the camel and there is the minaret let us see).

Used as a retort to a man who talks of an impossibility.

———

قط ملك ولا جمل شرك

A cat to oneself and not a camel in partnership.

———

عذاب ساعه ولا كل ساعه

Suffering for an hour but not suffering for every hour.

« *Better eye out than always aching.* »

———

الغريب اعمى ولو كان بصير

The stranger is blind, even though he see.

Said of one newly transferred from his usual occupation to one in which he is not yet experienced.

اللي يسرق بيضه يسرق جمل

He who steals an egg will steal a camel.

اصرف ما في الجيب يأتيك ما في الغيب

Spend what is in your pocket, there will come
what you may not expect.

« *Spend and God will send.* »

فار وقع من السما قال له القط اسم الله قال ابعد عني وانا بألف
خير من الله

A mouse fell from the roof. Said the cat : May
God guard thee ! Replied the mouse ; Keep thy distance and please God I am in excellent condition.

Quoted by one in misfortune who distrusts false sympathy.

كل صُدفه أخير من ميعاد

A chance meeting is better than an appointment.

قالوا للجمل النقارية جخ قال ياما دق على الدماغ طبول

They said « Boo » to (frighten) the camel carrying the drums. He said : What is this to the thumps
of the drums beaten over head.

A man under a great misfortune is insensible to a smaller
one.

ان كنت كذاب افتكر

If you are a liar recollect.

« *Liars should have good memories.* »

___

اللي ما ذاق اللحمه تعجبه الفشّه

He who never tasted meat will be contented
with lung.

___

كل واحد ينام على الجنب اللي يريحه

Every one sleeps on the side which gives him
most comfort.

« *Let every man play his own game.* »

___

واحد راح يصلّي لقى الجامع مقفول قال بركه يا جامع اللي جات
منك ما جات مني

One went to the mosque to say his prayers and
found it closed. He said : So much the better, O
mosque ! but it comes from you not from me.

Used by one who, when reluctantly resolved upon a good
act, is prevented from carrying it out, much to his own sa-
tisfaction.

___

القليل من البخيل كثير

Little from the miser is much.

ضحك من غير سبب قلّة ادب

A laugh without motive shows lack of education.
« *The loud laugh bespeaks the vacant mind.* »

———

راحت السكره وجات الفَكَرَه

Dissipation has passed and reflection has come.

Applied to one who, in a moment of excitement, has committed an act of folly, and who, upon returning to his sober senses, is the victim of remorse.

———

خد لك في كل بلد صاحب ولا في كل اقليم عدو

Take a friend in every town, but not an enemy in a province.

———

زبله وتقاوم الطيّار

A pigeon-dung, yet it tries to stem the current.
Running one's head against a stone wall. »

———

بصلة المحب خروف

An onion with a friend, is a (roast) lamb.

A modest repast is a feast where friendship prevails.

تكون في حنكك تقسم لغيرك

It may be in your mouth, yet it may fall to others.

« *There's many a slip 'twixt the cup and the lip.* »

الدنيا زي الغزّيه ترقص لكل واحد شويّه

The world is like the dancing girl, it dances before every one a little.

At an Egyptian feast, the dancing girl dances for a space before each guest in turn, paying marked attention, in the hope of obtaining a present. The proverb is quoted by a man to another as a token of sympathy in a misfortune that has befallen him.

ان كنت بدّك تتعلم ما تستحيش من السؤال

If you wish to learn, do not be bashful in asking questions.

يفتي على الابره ويبلع المدره

He delivers judgment upon a needle and swallows a pole.

« *He strains at a gnat and swallows a camel.* »

لا محبة الاّ بعد عداوة

No friendship except after enmity.

———

لاجل الورد ينسقي العليق

For the rose the thorn is watered.

A worthless fellow is often rendered a service out of regard for relatives or connections, as the thorn gets watered from its growing in proximity to a rose.

———

كل شي دواه الصبر لكن قلّة الصبر ما هاش دوا

Everything has a remedy in patience, but for the lack of patience there is no remedy.

———

حلم القطط كله فيران

The dreams of the cats are all of mice.

« *A lover dreams of his mistress.* »

———

زي حمير السكّه يتلزّز على قولة هشّ

Like the hired donkeys who rejoice at the word « Woa ».

Applied to a lazy fellow who works with reluctance and who, on the slightest pretext, will leave off working.

اليد اللي ما تقدرش تعضها بوسها

The hand that you cannot bite kiss.

ان كنتم اخوان تحاسبوا

If you are brothers keep accounts.

« *Short reckonings make long friends.* »

الاسم للنوره والفعل للزرنيخ

The name is for the depilatory and the action for the orpiment.

The depilatory called « Noorah » is often employed in the Arab baths. It is composed of quick-lime and an eighth part of orpiment made into a paste which removes superfluous hair when it is washed off. The proverb is said of one who has the credit whilst another has done the work.

السكوت اقرار

Silence gives consent.

بصل بخمسه والاّ بخمسه بصل

An onion for 5 (farthings) or 5 (farthings) for an onion.

« *Six of the one and half a dozen of the other* ».

اللي صباعه في المَيَّه مُش زي اللي صباعه في النار

He whose finger is in the water is not like him whose finger is in the fire.

Quoted by one in adversity to a friend who regards his trouble with equanimity.

———

اترك الذنب ولا تطلب المغفره

Avoid the fault and you will not have to ask pardon.

———

ست وجاريتين على قلي بيضتين

The mistress and two slaves for frying two eggs.

« *Much ado about nothing.* »

———

من دمى سلاحه حُرِم قتله

To put to death one who renders up his arms is unlawful.

One who openly confesses should be treated with clemency.

———

الوِحده ولا القرين السوء

Solitude is preferable to a bad companion.

الهروب نصف الشطاره

Flight is half wisdom.

Said half in praise half in ridicule.

> « *He who fights and runs away*
> *Lives to fight another day.* »

الحجر الداير لا بد له من لطّه

A stone turning is sure to be chipped.

Meaning that a man of dissolute habits is sure someday to regret it. Also that one constantly doing wrong is sure to be detected.

فقير وكلامه كتير

Poor and yet he talks much.

ان كان عندك نحس ما تسيبوش لحَسَنْ يجيلك انحس منه

If you have a worthless (friend or servant) do not part with him for fear of getting a worse.

> « *Better the ills we know than those we know not of.* »

اللسان ترجمان القلب

The tongue is the interpreter of the heart.

عقلك في راسك تعرف خلاصك

You have your own mind, do as you please.

Said to one by his friend who persists in an action, contrary to his friend's warning that ill may come of it.

———

من يمدح العروسه الاّ امها وابوها

Who praises the bride, if it be not her mother and father?

« *Every potter cracks up his own vessel* ».

———

احسب حساب المريسي وان جا الطياب من الله

Calculate upon a south wind and if the north wind blows it will be a Godsend.

To ascend the Nile a northerly wind is essential; in descending the sail may be taken in and the barque allowed to drift with the current. The proverb is used as a recommendation to be prepared for the worst in any transaction, then if all goes well it will be the more appreciated.

———

اللي عنده حنّه يحني ديل حماره

He who has (abundance) of « hennah » may stain his donkey's tail.

« *They that have good store of butter may put some in their shoes* ».

قدح جاه ولا وية مال

An ounce of power and not a ton of wealth.

———

جحا عمل ساقيه تمى من البحر وتكبّ فيهِ تاني قالوا له ايه الفائده
قال يكفيني نعيرها

Goha constructed a water-wheel to draw water
from the river and to pour it back again. They said
to him : What is the advantage of this ? He said : Its
creaking is sufficient for me.

Used to signify the pleasure of possession even though the
thing possessed be useless.

———

الكذب داء والصدق شفاء

Falsehood is sickness and truth is health.

———

زي عزومة المراكبية

Like the invitation of the (passing) boatmen.

The Nile boatmen, whenever meeting and passing in different directions on the Nile invariably hail and invite each
other to come and eat, a mere custom with no meaning at-
tached to it on either side ; hence the expression is quoted
upon receiving a hollow invitation.

زي العطّار الاهبل يحفظ الورق ويبعزق المستكه

Like the silly druggist, he preserves the (packing) paper and scatters the gum-mastic.

« *Penny wise and pound foolish* ».

الفضل للمبتدي وان احسن المقتدي

The merit belongs to the beginner even if the follower does better.

المكسب في الوحْل ولا الخساره في المسك

A profit in dirt rather than a loss in musk.

يغرق في شبر ميّه

He gets drowned in a span of water.

Applied to a man incapable of helping himself or any one else.

كلب فالت ولا سبع مربوط

A dog loose rather than a lion chained.

ان ولّعت لك العشره ما تشوفهم الآ ظلام

If I lit for you the ten (fingers, as candles) you
would regard them as if they were in darkness.

« *Where there is no love, all are faults* ».

———

الكلاب ما يعضش في ودن اخوه

The dog does not bite the ear of another dog.

An expression much used, and applied to one who defends
his absent friend from the aspersion of the company.

———

يا ما في الحبس من مظاليم

How many in prison are there : unjustly.

———

اللي يعمل جمل ما يبعبعش من العمل

He who makes himself a camel must not grumble
at the burden.

Said to one who after boasting of his capacity grumbles
at the work put upon him.

———

امسك القطه تخربشك

Catch the cat and she will scratch yo

Said to one who has been rebuffed for
with a cross-grained individual.

القرد في عين امه غـزال

The baboon, in the eyes of its mother, is a gazelle.

« *Every mother thinks her own goose a swan* »

الدنيا ما خلقتش في يوم

The world was not created in a day.

« *Rome was not built in a day* ».

مال تجيبه الرياح تأخذهُ الزوابع

Wealth brought by the wind is scattered by the hurricane.

« *Easy come easy go* ».

الحق مرّ

Truth is bitter.

قطته جمل

His cat is a camel.

« *All his geese are swans* ».

راح يخطبها له اتجوزها..

He (the matchmaker) went to engage her (for another) and he married her.

Said of one who being commissioned to arrange a matter transacts the business for his own profit.

الخساره تعلّم الشطاره

Loss teaches wisdom.

العجلة من الشيطان

Haste is of the devil.

« *More haste worse speed* ».

امسك على الحبل يدلك على الحمار

Catch the halter-rope and it will lead you to the donkey.

If you want to get at the root of a matter commence at its origin.

اللي يتلف شيء عليه اصلاحه

He who destroys a thing should repair it.

زمار الحارة ما يطربش

The reed-player of (your own) street does not charm.

« *No one is a prophet in his own country* ».

جيت ادعي عليه لقيت الحيطه مايله عليه

I was about to call God's wrath upon him when I saw the wall leaning towards him.

Used to signify that it is not worth while to seek to injure a man already on the brink of destruction.

———

اذا أردت ان تطاع فاسأل ما يستطاع

If you would be obeyed ask what is feasible.

———

يقول للحرامي اسرق ولصاحب البيت استحرص

He tells the thief to steal and the owner of the house to beware.

« *To hunt with the hounds and run with the hare* ».

———

الدراهم مراهم

Money is a salve.

خد بايدي اليوم أخد برجلك بكره

Take me by the hand to-day and I will take
you by the leg to-morrow.

Used to express that for a small service rendered, a greater
will be returned.

قبل ما يشتري البقرة بنى المدود

Before buying the cow he built the manger.

« Do not count your chickens before they are
hatched ».

قالو يابختك يا ديك من البيضه للحمره قال والله ما يخي دا كله في
سحبة السكينة

They said : oh lucky cock. From the white to the
red (hen). He replied : By God, what is all this to
the drawing of the knife.

٠. man envies his friend his good fortune without consi-
dering that there may be drawbacks to his position.

ما دام الراس سالم البدن سالم

As long as the head is well the body is well.

« When the head acheth all the body is the
orse ».

ان ما كانش فيه وفاق ففراق

If there is no accord, better to separate.

الرجال عند اغراضها نسوان

Men, when they desire a thing, become like women.

In the East, a woman is supposed to lead a life of subserviency, hence a man is likened to a women when he becomes subservient.

كتر العتاب يورث البغض

Too many reproaches beget animosity.

راس الكسلان بيت الشيطان

The head of the lazy is the house of the devil.

« *Satan finds some mischief still for idle hands to do* ».

وحشه ولاده احسن من حلوه عاقر

An ugly woman fruitful rather than a pretty woman sterile.

اللي له ظهر ما ينضربش على بطنه

He who has a back (to protect him) will not be
struck in his stomach.

A man menaced with a blow in the stomach which would
be serious, if not fatal but for the interposition of a friend's
back upon which the blow falls. The proverb means that one
in trouble, if powerfully protected, need not fear for his
position.

الحمار في دماغه صوت ما يستريحش الا لما يزعقه

The donkey has a sound in his head; he is
uneasy till rid of it.

« *Every ass loves to hear himself bray* ».

يضربني في زفه ويصالحني في عطفه

He beats me in a procession and makes peace
with me in a bye-way.

Applied commonly to one who is insolent when many are
about, counting on their interposition, but humble when
alone and unaided.

الف عدو برا الدار ولا عدو جو الدار

A thousand enemies without the house and not
one within.

ما كل مرَّة تسلم الجرَّة

It is not every time that the pitcher is saved.

« *The pitcher that goes often to the well comes home broken at last* ».

———

ركبته ورايه حط ايده في الخرج

I gave him a ride behind me and he put his hand in the saddle-bags.

Ingratitude. Returning evil for good.

———

البياض نصف الجمال

Fairness is half the beauty.

———

شبيه الشيء منجذب اليه

Like is attracted by like.

« *Birds of a feather flock together* ».

———

ضل راجل ولا ضل حيط

The shadow of a man and not the shadow of a wall.

An expression used to induce a girl to get married.

طالب المال بلا مال كحامل الماء في غربال

He who covets wealth without means, is like him
who would carry water in a sieve.

———

زي هزار الحمير عض ورفص

Like the play of the donkeys. biting and kicking.

« *Jest with an ass and he will flap you in the
face with his tail* ».

———

قالوا للفأر خد محبوب وامشي على شنب القطه قال الاجرة طيبة بس في
الطريق مشقة

They told the mouse to take a guinea and walk
on the moustaches of the cat. He said : the pay is
good, but the path is troublesome.

The reply of a man to whom a proposition is made in-
volving too much risk.

———

اللي تطلعه السمره تضيعه على الخطوط والحمرة

What the brunette gains, she spends in cos-
metics.

« *Fair faces need no paint* »

الحق اللي وراه مطالب ما يموتش

A right with a claimant does not die out.

المكسب يقوي القلب

Profit emboldens the heart.

كلها يوم وليله و يجي الحج الرميلة

It is but a day and a night and the pilgrims ca‑
ravan will arrive at Romela.

Romela (Menshiyah nowadays), situated at the foot of the
Citadel of Cairo, is the starting place of the Mahmal or Holy
carpet for Mecca and where this carpet is brought after
covering the prophet's tomb at Mecca for a year. The saying is
commonly used to council patience. A day and a night only
and the long wearisome journey will have come to an end.

الحاجه اللي ما تهمك وصي عليها جوز امك

What you do not much care for, you may en‑
trust to your step-father.

Divorces in Egypt not being unfrequent, the husband of
the mother is most likely not the child's father, and as gene‑
rally happens, there is no love lost between them. Quoted as a
reproach to one who, from indifference, has not carried out
what was entrusted to him.

لبس البوصه تبقى عروسه

Dress the reed and it will resemble a bride.

« *Fine feathers make fine birds* ».

فقر وحماقة ما ينفقوش

Poverty and anger do not agree.

القامه مصقولة وما في الجيب فوله

Erect of stature and not a bean in his pocket.

« *Poor but proud* ».

عيشك حلو يا خالتى قالت من سوء بختي يا بنت اختي

Oh my aunt, your bread is so sweet! She said : It is my bad luck, oh daughter of my sister.

Applied to one who thrusts himself where he is not welcome.

اضرب الطينه في الحيط ان ما لزقت اثرت

Throw mud upon a wall ; if it does not stick, it will leave a mark.

امشى سنه ولا تخطي قنا

Walk for a year and cross not a water-course.

« *Better go round than fall into the ditch* ».

بلاش تطعمني فرخة سمينه وتبيتني حزينة

Do not feed me with a fat hen and make me sleep uneasily.

Said by a wife to her husband who, though providing for her creature comforts, is otherwise indifferent. It is also applied to an employer who, though liberal as to payment, abuses his servant.

كل كلب ينبح ما يعضش

Every dog that barks does not bite.

الحيطان دفاتر المجانين

The walls are the registers of fools.

« *White walls are fool's writing paper* ».

ديل الكلب عمره ما ينعدل

A dog's tail is never straight.

Applied to one whose misconduct is invariable.

كلب أحى ولا سبع ميت

A live dog better than a dead lion.

الكلمة اللينة تكسر الغضب

A mild word turns away wrath.

« *A soft answer turneth away wrath* ».

Proverbs XV. — I.

يا اللي شاف التايهة ذال ان شا الله اللي خدها يندبح بها قال وايش عرفك انها سكينة

Who has seen it ? One answered : Would to God whoever saw it may be slain by it. He (the questioner) said : How did you know it was a knife.

Said to one who, out of his own mouth, convicts himself.

كل عقدة لها عند الكريم حلال

Every knot has an unraveller in God.

الكلام كلام علما والفعل فعل ابليس

The words are those of the wise; the deeds are those of devils.

اتغدى واتمدى ولو دقيقتين واتعشى واتمشى ولو خطوتين

Dine and recline if for two minutes ; sup and walk if for two paces.

« *After dinner sit a while*
After supper walk a mile. »

عينه فيه وتفوه عليه

He has his eyes upon it and yet he spits upon it.

Said of one who covets a thing whilst affecting to despise it.

خذوا اخباركم من صغاركم

Take your news from the little ones.

« *What the children hear at home soon flies abroad* ».

من دوّر على شيء لقاه

Who seeks a thing finds it.

اللي ما يستحي يفعل ما يشتهي

Who is without shame will do as he likes (without regard to others).

اردب ما هو لك ما تحضر كيله تتغبر ذقنك وما ينوبك الا شيله

When an «Ardab» (of corn) which does not be-
long to you is measured do not be present, for your
beard will be dusty and you may have to carry it.

Do not interfere in what does not concern you, for it
may get you into trouble.

An « Ardeb » is equivalent, very nearly, to five English
bushels.

اللي ما يعرفك يجهلك

Who does not know you ignores you.

Said in excuse to one who had been harshly treated
before his identity became known.

اللي ما يشوفش من الغربال اعمى

Who does not see through the sieve is blind.

« *There are none so blind as those who will
not see* ».

ما كامل الا محمد

Nobody is perfect save Mohamed.

Used by a Mohamedan in reply to a friend's censure
upon his pet vice.

اللي تملكه اليد تكرهه النفس

What the hand possesses palls upon the soul.

« *Possession begets satiety* »

بدال ما تغشه قول له في وشه

Instead of deceiving him tell him to his face.

بعيد عن العين بعيد القلب

Far from the sight, far from the heart.

« *Out of sight out of mind* ».

قيراط سعد ولا فدان شطارة

A « Kirat » of luck and not a « feddan » of ability.

A « kirat » is a very small patch of ground, a « feddan » is approximately equal to an acre. The proverb is applied to one who invariably succeeds although seemingly devoid of intelligence.

خذ من الغريم ولو حجر

Take from your debtor even a stone.

ما يمدح السوق الا اللي ربح فيه

Who gains in the market extols it.

« *Let every man praise the bridge he goes over* ».

———

ابوك خلف لك ايه قال جدي ومات

What has your father left you? He replied a
he-goat and it died.

A company of friends sat down to eat. One of them
asked another, not the most intelligent of the party, what he
had inherited : whereupon he narrated a long story which
was not finished till the last dish was brought ; then, seeking
to avenge himself, he asked the same question of another
who replied briefly as above, in order not to lose his share
of the repast. Hence the proverb is frequently used to denote
reluctance to being questioned.

———

اللي بيته من قزاز ما يرجمش الناس بالحجارة

He whose house is of glass must not throw stones
at others.

———

شعره من هنا وشعره من هناك يعملوادقن

A hair from here, a hair from there, will make
a beard.

« *Many a mickle makes a muckle* ».

يا بنتي خايفه عليك من العيلة قالت يا امي لساني معايه

O my daughter! I am anxious for you on account
of his family. She replied ; O my mother, I have my
tongue.

Maternal solicitude on the eve of a daughter's marriage.
One about to transact business with an astute person, on
being warned by his friend to be careful, quotes the proverb
to indicate that he considers himself equal to the occasion.

اتكلموا باحسان لَحْسن الحيطان لها ودان

Speak cautiously, for walls have ears.

الكذب مالوش رجلين

Falsehood has no legs.

« *A liar cannot escape detection* ».

جا يكحلها عماها

In « kohling » her (eyes) he blinded her.

In rendering a service he unintentionally did an injury.

الايد الواحده ما تزقفش

One hand cannot applaud.

Need of cooperation.

خطبوها اتعززت فاتوها اتندمت

When engaged she was coy, when freed she re-
pented.

An offer not appreciated till withdrawn.

————

البير الحلو دائماً نازح

A well of sweet water is always empty.

Applied to one whose generosity leaves him frequently
penniless.

————

اللي في قلبه على طرف لسانه

What is in his heart is on the tip of his tongue.

Applied to one whose natural candour obliges him to give
utterance to his thought.

————

الباب اللي يجي لك منه الريح سده واستريح

Close the door from which comes the draught,
and be tranquil.

Get rid of the source of your discomfort and make no
more ado about it.

اتبع البوم يوديك الخراب

Follow the owl, it will lead you to a ruin.

Illustrative of the evil of bad company.

الدرهم الايض ينفع في النهار الاسود

The white coins will serve in the black day.

The results of economy will be serviceable in adversity.

بعد ما راح المقبره بقي في حنكه سكره

After he went to the tomb (i. e. died), you find that he had sugar in his mouth.

Said to one who, after having broken with his friend, discovers his merits.

الكلام لكي يا جاره بس انت حماره

The words are (addressed) to you, oh neighbour, only you are a she-ass.

Quoted to one who pretends not to understand remarks made against him.

سد ودن بطينة والثانيه بعجينه

Stop one ear with mud and the other with paste.

An advice to pay no attention to disagreeable remarks.

زَعَلَه على طرف مناخيره

His anger is at the tip of his nose.

Said of a quick tempered man.

خبطتين على الراس توجع

Two blows on the head will hurt.

One misfortune may be supportable, but two over whelming.

ضَرِبة في كيس غيرك كانها في تل رمل

A blow on the purse of another is like a blow on a sand-hill.

Any thing that does not affect oneself is easy to bear.

اللي ياكلهم مش زي اللي يعدهم

He who receives the blows is not like him who counts them.

A witness, however sympathetic, cannot feel like the sufferer.

من طقطق للسلام عليكم

From knocking till Good-bye.

Signifying from beginning to end.

اصبر على جارك السوء يا يرحل ياتجي له داهيه

Be patient with your mischievous neighbour; he
may either quit or get the plague.

Said to one who is annoyed by another whom time may
some day remove in one way or another.

ناموسه باتت على شجره قالت لها الصبح امسكي روحك احسن انا طايره

A mosquito slept on a tree. In the morning she
said to the tree: take care I am going to fly.

Applied to one who thinks his most trivial action is of
importance to others.

الرجل تدبّ مطرح ما تحبّ

The foot treads where you love.

Meaning that a person frequents only the abode of one for
whom he has love and esteem.

البلاش كثر منه

Of that which costs (me) nothing give (me) plenty.

Said to one who takes to excess that which he gets for
nothing.

قبل ما يشوفوه يقولوا كويس زي ابوه

Before they see him, they say he is as handsome
as his father.

Said of a child not yet born. Generally applied to those
who laud one before acquaintances.

اكبر منك بيوم يعرف اكثر منك بسنه

Older than you by a day, wiser than you by a
year.

قالوا يا جحا امراة ابوك تحبك قال يبقى تجننت

They said : O Goha, the wife of your father loves
you. He replied : She is gone mad then.

The ill will of the step-mother is generally acknowledged.

زي العالمه تتبغدد في بيت الزبون

Like the female-singer who gives herself airs in
the client's house.

The principal singers in Egypt know that their services
at a feast are indispensable and they give themselves great airs
in consequence, and the proverb is quoted to one who, in
return for the hospitality he receives, makes himself disagreeable.

اسأل مجرَّب ولا تسأل طبيب

Ask from the experienced rather than from the physician.

Intended to convey the idea that practical knowledge is better than theory.

———

ما تفرحش للي راح لما تشوف اللي يجي

Do not rejoice over him who goes, before you see him who comes.

However objectionable may be the one who is leaving, he may be succeeded by one more objectionable still.

———

اعزّ ايامك ايه يا جحا قال لما كنت أعبي التراب في الطقيه

When were your happiest days, oh Goha? He replied : when I filled my cap with earth.

The children of poor people wear white cotton caps and they amuse themselves by filling them with earth, as children in the West amuse themselves by making mud pies.

———

خبر بجديد قال بكره يبقى بلاش

(One cried) The news for a farthing ! Another answered : to-morrow it will be for nothing.

Quoted to one unwilling to impart information which must sooner or later be made public.

المداوي القديم مرحوم

The old ferryman is blessed.

Frequently used in reference to a chief who has retired, he being succeeded by one still more exacting.

———

جور الترك ولا عدل العرب

The oppression of the Turks rather than the justice of the Arabs.

———

قالو للقطه وسخك دوا خنت ودفنته

They said to the cat : your excrement is a remedy : She made a hole and buried it.

Quoted to one who will not render a service, though having the means of doing so.

———

قالوا للقاضي حيطه شخ عليها الكلاب قال لازم هدّها قالوا دي اللي بيننا وبينكم قال قليل من الماء يطهرها

They told the Qadi : A dog has defiled the wall. The Qadi said : Knock it down. But said they : it is the division wall between you and us. Oh ! replied the Qadi : a little water then will purify it.

Self-interest modifying one's views.

انا خابزه وعاجنه

I have baked him and kneaded him.

Referring to one known intimately to you.

———

لو كان الاسم ينشرى لكان الفلاح سمّى ابنه وحل

If the name had to be bought, the Fellah would name his son « dirt ».

Showing the thrift of the Egyptian peasant.

———

ما شاتمك الا من بلغك

Your insulter is he who brings you the report.

« *He who repeats the ill he hears of another is the true slanderer* ».

———

ترمس امبابه احسن من اللوز قال ده جبر خاطر للفقراء

The lupins of Embabeh are better than almonds : He said : (oh no !) That is but a consolation for the poor (who cannot afford buying almonds).

The lupins of Embabeh, a village opposite Cairo, on the West bank of the Nile, are famous throughout Egypt, but they are not of course to be compared to almonds, and the proverb is quoted by one who endeavours to content himself with what is within his means.

سكة ابو زيد كلها مسالك

To Abu-Zeid's there are many paths.

« *All roads lead to Rome* »

راحت اخذ بتثار ابوها رجعت حبله

She went to revenge her father and returned pregnant.

Said of a person who goes to quarrel with somebody but ends by becoming his friend.

لو لا الذنب ما كانت المغفره

If there were no fault, there would be no pardon.

Quoted to one who hesitates in accepting a proferred excuse for an offence.

ثلاثة اذا اتفقوا على بلد يخربوها

Three, if united against a village, will ruin it.

Referring to the power of combination for evil as well as for good.

الولد البطال يجيب لاهله اللعنه

The bad boy is a curse to his parents.

اجتمع المتعوس على خايب الرجا

The unlucky and the hopeless have met.

A saying, often addressed in fun to two friends when found together by an acquaintance.

عرايا مققفين جابوا بعشاهم ياسمين

Naked and shivering, yet with the price of their supper they bought jasmin.

Said of those who spend their money foolishly.

كل فيه يآلم بس مبلعه سالم

Everything ails him except his swallow.

Said of one who shams sickness.

اللي مالوش حد له ربنا

He who has no friend has God.

Said by one in need of assistance.

حسبنا في القبه شيخ

We thought there was a saint under the dome.

A dome indicates the burying place of a « Sheikh » or holy man and the proverb is quoted by one who has been misled by externals.

اكوي على الخبر ماجور

Cover this news with an earthenware vessel.

Used by one who has made a communication to his friend and wishes to enjoin secrecy.

موت يا حمار لما يجي لك العليق

Die, oh donkey, till the fodder arrives.

One seeking help and being put off for a period, quotes the above, meaning that he will have to suffer in the mean-time.

زي ابن العنزه يعيط وفي حنكه البزّ

Like the lamb that bleats with the teat in its mouth.

Applied to one constantly grumbling without reason.

خميرة جارك ما تخمرش عيشك

The yeast of your neighbour will not make your bread rise.

Quoted to one who would count upon others for what he should do for himself.

ان كان في قلعك ريح افضه

If you have wind in your sail shake it out.

A scornful reply to an idle threat.

ما واحدة على الكوم لما شافت لها يوم

No one upon the mound who has not seen a (happy) day.

Women of the lowest class or of bad repute in Cairo were obliged to dwell upon the rubbish mounds near the town and the above is quoted to indicate however miserable any one's present position may be, he must have spent some happy days.

شابت لحاهم والعقل لسا ما جاهم

Their beards have grown white and yet wisdom has not yet come to them.

Applied to one to whom time and experience bring no knowledge.

السلطان ينشتم في غيته

The Sultan is vilified in his absence.

Said to appease one who complains that during his absence he has been ill spoken of.

اللي عنده حمار اعرج احسن من اللي ما عندوش

He who has a lame donkey is better off than he who has none.

The donkey being almost universally employed by the Egyptian peasants as a means of locomotion and transport, no one will walk from one village to another who possesses even a maimed animal.

عمر التشفيط ما يملي قرب

Little drops will not fill a water skin.

Said in reply to an exhortation to be saving on small means.

احنا خير ما عملنا من أين الشر جا لنا

Good have we not done, whence comes this evil,

A reflection on the tendency to return evil for good.

اللي ما تربيه امه وابوه تربيه الايام والليالي

Him whom his father and mother have not educated, the days and nights will educate.

Said of one who, not having had his faults corrected by his parents, will learn by experience.

ان كه هك جا لك حول باب دارك

If your neighbour dislikes you, change your entrance.

———

القلب ما ساعش اتنين

The heart cannot hold two.

———

زي البقه تولد كل يوم ميه وتقول يا قلة الذريه

Like the bug that produces a hundred daily and exclaims : oh lack of offspring.

Said of a mother of many children still desirous of more. Also of one who is never satisfied whatever he is granted.

———

جمل بارك من عياه قال حملوه يتوم

A camel is lying down from illness. They said : put a burden upon him and he will rise.

Said ironically by one already over-burthened with work, at a fresh demand upon his endurance.

———

اللي يعقد عقده يعرف يحلها

He who ties a knot can undo it.

Said to an official who has so wantonly complicated an affair that he only can unravel it.

كل نومه وتطيطه احسن من فرح طيطه

Every sleep and yawn is better than attending a marriage of Tita.

Tita is said to have been a rich Copt and renowned for the splendour of the festivities he gave on the marriages of his children, and the proverb is quoted in reply to an invitation which would be inconvenient to accept.

لما يقع النصيب من السما يبلى الخطاب بالعمى

When your lot falls from heaven, the match-maker is struck with blindness.

Said to console one who has married a plain bride, the match-maker having represented her as lovely.

ما للحب المسوس الاكيال اعور

For worm-eaten grain a one-eyed measurer.

Applied to two friends whose mutual defects seem to render them suited to each other.

سألوا البغل من ابوك قال خالي الحصان

They asked the mule: who is your father? He said: my uncle is a horse.

Applied to one who by giving an indirect answer, avoids committing himself.

اللي تخوضه انت يفرق فيه غيرك

What you can ford yourself may drown others.

A difficulty that you may easily surmount may prove fatal
to another.

———

حداية ضَمّنت غراب قال يطيرو١ الا ثنين

A kite would become guarantee for a crow. They
said : they would fly away together.

Quoted to a man without means wishing to guarantee
another penniless man.

———

حبيبك اللي يحزن لحزنك وعدوك اللي يفرح في مصيبتك

Your friend is he who grieves at your griefs and
your enemy is he who rejoices at your misfortune.

———

الطَمع اضاع ما جمع

Greed will lose what has been amassed.

« Grasp all lose all ».

———

عند الشدّة تعرف الاخوان

In adversity the friends are known.

« Adversity tries friends ».

زي فوطة الحمّام كل ساعة في وسط راجل

Like the towel of a (public Turkish) bath, every hour it girdles a different man's waist.

Said of a Mohammedan woman who has been often divorced.

يا واخد القرد على ماله يروح المال ويبقى القرد على حاله

Oh you who have taken a monkey for his wealth, the wealth will disappear and the monkey remain as before.

Quoted to a man who would marry for money, neglecting beauty and accomplishments.

بعد نومك ويا الجديان بقى لك مطلّ على الجيران

After sleeping with the goats, you have now a window overlooking the neighbours.

Said to one who has risen from extreme poverty to affluence.

اللي يتكلم في ما لا يعنيه يسمع ما لا يرضيه

He who talks about what does not concern him will hear what does not please him.

الضرب في الميت حرام

Beating the dead is a sin.

Meaning it is useless to reproach a man with no feelings. Also useless to seek payment from a penniless man.

———

اللي يزعل نسلخ وشه

Of him who gets angry we will skin the face.

Often used by one friend to another who is beginning to lose his temper at a remark made by a third person present.

———

قال ايش حاجزك عن الرقص قال قصر الاكمام

What prevents you from dancing ? He replied : The shortness of the sleeves.

Said by one who, wishing to embark upon an enterprise or speculation, is prevented from want of means.

———

اللي تعرفه احسن من اللي ما تعرفوش

He whom you know is better than he whom you do not know.

Quoted to recommend forbearance in cases where someone wishes to dismiss a servant for a new one.

حسبنا حساب الحيّه اما العقرب ما كانتش على البال

We were prepared for the serpent but gave no thought to the scorpion.

We were prepared for the palpable but not for the hidden danger.

———

قالوا للحرامي احلف قال جا الفرَج

They told the thief to swear : He said (to himself) : Liberation is approaching.

Said by one in trouble and who will hesitate at nothing in order to get out of the difficulty.

———

خاطر الاعمى قفه عيون

The desire of a blind-man is for a basketful of eyes.

The reply of one who is offered what he has a great desire for.

———

لا تعامل المجنون ولا تخلّي المجنون يعاملك

Do not deal with the mad and do not let the mad deal with you.

That is, have no dealings with rogues.

اضرب البري لما يقرّ المتهوم

Beat the innocent until the suspected confesses.

Used to imply that cunning and duplicity are essential for a man to arrive at the truth.

———

ضربته والقبر

A blow from him and the grave.

Applied to a man of a ferocious character : also to an usurer whose rates of interest are killing.

———

كل راس مطاطيه تحتها الف بليَّه

Under every down-hanging head dwell a thousand mischiefs.

The habit of bending the head in token of servility is taken as a sign of evil design.

———

العاقل يحت ويدفن والجاهل يغسل وينشر

The wise will dig and bury ; the fool will wash and display.

Said in illustration of thrift and extravagance.

القرْص بغض ولو كان من ايد فضه والعض محبه ولو كان من بوز كلبه

Pinching is enmity even from a silver finger and
biting is affection even from a dog's mouth.

اللي يعمل نفسه نخاله تأكله الخنازير

Him who makes himself bran, the swine will eat

He who does not maintain his position will not be
respected.

النعجة العيّاطه ما ياكلش ابنها الديب

The wolf will not attack the lamb of the bleat-
ing sheep.

Generally applied to one who escaped mishap (such as
the loss of his post) by the importunities of his relatives or
friends.

زي المراكبية ما يفتكروش ربنا الاّ وقت الغرق

Like the sailors who only pray when about to
be wrecked.

Quoted to one who, in his prosperity, was arrogant:
misfortune arising he abases himself to those he formerly
neglected.

رحنا نساعده في دفن ابوه فات لنا الفاس ومشى

We went to help him to bury his father ; he left
his spade and went away.

Said of one who induces his friend to participate in his
difficulty and then leaves him in the lurch.

———

شراره تحرق حاره

A spark may burn a street.

———

يلاقي عظم في الفشه

He finds bone in lung.

Lung is eaten by the poorer classes in the towns and the
proverb is applied to a man proverbially unlucky.

———

جم يحلبوا قرده كشّت قالوا يغور اللبن اللي يجي من وشك

They came to milk a she-monkey. She drew back
coyly. They said : Let the milk that comes from one
with your face go to the devil.

A favor granted ungraciously is accepted with aversion or
rejected with scorn.

الارتباك علامة على الارتكاب

Confusion is a sign of guilt.

Applied to one under interrogation whose answers are given with hesitation. Also to a Government scribe who unnecessarily prolongs and complicates a simple matter for the purpose of obtaining a present.

قال ياجحا الحرامي في بيتكم قال ما هوش بعيد عن صندوقي

Oh Goha. A thief is in your house. He said : Is he not far from my trunk ?

Said by one who, so long as that which belongs to him is not touched, is indifferent as to what may occur to the property of others.

قمر وزيت دا خراب بيت

Moonlight and oil (together) are the ruin of a house.

« *Burning the candle at both ends* »

شَرَبه من برَّه توفر الجرَّه

A drink outside will save the pitcher.

As water is carried in pitchers by women from the Nile or a Canal frequently at a distance from their village, this saying is used to inculcate forethought.

زي حمار الغزيّه يسمع الطبلة يهزّ وسطه

Like the donkey of the dancing-girl, on hearing
the drum it wags its hind quarters.

The « Ghaziah » or dancing-girl is nearly always accom-
panied by a small donkey used for carrying the instruments
and it sometimes performs to the sound of the « Darabokka »
or drum. The proverb is used to signify that habit becomes a
second nature.

ما يمسح دمعتك الّا إيدك

Nothing wipes your tears away but your own
hand.

Self-dependence.

البشاشة ولا اكل العيش

Affability rather than eating bread.

« *It is a sin against hospitality to open your
door and shut up your countenance* ».

اقول لك طواشي تقول لي اولاده كم

I tell you he is a eunuch, you ask me how many
children he has.

Quoted to one who makes an irrelevant reply.

على باب الاطرش قد ما تحب خبَّط

At the door of a deaf man you may knock as long as you like.

Said to one who has vainly sought a service from a notoriously indolent or effete person.

———

ان كان لك عند الكلب حاجه قول له يا سيدي

If you owe a dog anything, call him « Sir ».

———

ما ينعملش كيس حرير من ودن خانزير

A silk purse cannot be made out of a sow's ear.

———

اتعلم الادب من قليل الادب

Learn politeness from the impolite.

« *Learn wisdom by the follies of others* ».

———

كل نومه على القلاقيل مرتاحه أحسن من مخدّه وترّاحه

All sleep on the clods with comfort is better than on a pillow and mattress.

Poverty with tranquillity rather than riches with anxiety.

من إدّاين العيش اعذروه ومن إدّاين اللحم الطشوه

He who owes for bread excuse him,
He who owes for meat (also) beat him.

Quoted by one in reply to a reproach upon his indebtedness to show that he has incurred no debt upon luxuries.

غلا وسوء كيل

Dearness, yet false measure.

Generally said to a merchant who charges exorbitantly and at the same time endeavours to cheat.

الطشاش ولا العمى

Rather shortsight than blindness.

« *Half a loaf is better than no bread* ».

سكينة الاهل مثلّمه

The knife of relatives is blunt.

Applied in the same sense as « Blood is thicker than water ».

ان كنتِ وحشه كوني نغشه

If you are ugly, be winsome.

زيّ حيَّه تحت تِبن

Like a snake under the straw.

Bearing the same significance as the English «Like a snake in the grass».

———

ورّي عذرك ولا تورّي بخلك

Show your reason rather than be thought avaricious.

It is better to avow your inability to comply with a request than be thought mean.

———

الجابي مبغوض

The collector is (always) hated.

Especially so in Egypt, as it is obligatory for a new tenant on his first arrival to pay the amount of a month's rent in advance to the rent-collector upon the delivery of the key of the house or flat. This demand is called « Muftahiah » or key-tax·

———

العريان في القافله مرتاح

The naked in a caravan enjoys tranquillity.

Having nothing to lose, he need not concern himself about robbers during the journey.

« *The beggar may sing before the thief* ».

الطلب اللين يضيّع الحق البيّن

A lenient demand destroys a strong right.

« *When the demand is a jest, the fittest answer is a scoff* ».

باتت جيعانه وجوزها خبّاز

She went hungry to bed, though her husband is a baker.

Applied in cases of needless suffering.

عاشر المتهوم تنتهم

Frequent the suspected you will be suspected.

« *A man is known by the company he keeps* »

ثور الحرث ما يتكمّش

The ox that is ploughing is not to be muzzled.

« *Thou shalt not muzzle the ox that treadeth out the corn* ». Scrip.

كل ممنوع حلو

Everything forbidden is sweet.

« *Forbidden fruit is sweet* ».

عزموا ثور على فرح قال يا للساقيه يا للطاحون

They invited an ox to a wedding. He said : Is it
to turn the water-wheel or the mill.

Said by one who suspects that he is to be entertained for
an ulterior motive.

الدبان يعرف وش اللبان

The flies know the face of the milkman.

Said of one who knows where to go for what he wants.

زي المالطي كل ما يكبر يتجنن

Like the Maltese, the older he grows the madder
he becomes.

Said of a man or boy who does not grow wiser as he
grows older.

بوس الايادي ضحك على الدقون

Kissing the hands is laughing at the beards.

Said of a man who flatters another to get something by
him.

حماتك مناقرة قال طلّق بنتها

Your mother-in-law is quarrelsome. He said :
Divorce her daughter.

Meaning that there is always a way out of a difficulty.

———

قال كفّنه واعمل له عمّه قالــ انا مغسّل وضامن جنّه

He said : Put him in his shroud and wind his tur-
ban. He replied : Am I a corpse-washer and para-
dise ensurer.

Said in reply to a request for two services widely
different.

———

زي الجوار كل ما يكبروا يخسّوا في الثمن

Like the female slaves, the older they grow the
less their value.

———

اطعم الفم تستحي العين

Feed the mouth, the eye will be bashful.

Give a bribe and the delinquency will be passed over.

العذر اقبح من الذنب

The excuse is worse than the fault.

Quoted to one who aggravates his offence by lame excuses.

قالوا للسلطان الناس جواعه قال خليهم ياكلوا بقلاوه

They said to the Sultan : the people are starving :
He said : Let them eat pastry.

Said of one who ignorantly judges of another's circumstances by his own.

اكل الدقه والنوم في الازقه ولا فرخه محمره يعقبها مشقه

Eating « Doqqah » and sleeping in the bye-lanes,
rather than a roast hen followed by fatigue.

The « Doqqah » is a cheap mixture of pounded seed,
(cumin, wild marjoram, or mint) salt and pepper, for flavour-
ing the bread.

Better the tranquillity of a modest competence than the
trouble of riches.

يوديك البحر ويجيبك عطشان

He can lead you to the river and bring you back
thirsty.

« *He can twist you round his little finger* ».

الدلال القليل البخت لايعجب البايع ولا الشاري

The unlucky auctioneer pleases neither the seller nor the buyer.

Said of one who intervenes between two and pleases neither.

———

وقيّة ليّة ولا رطل كرشه

An ounce of fat rather than a pound of tripe.

A small thing that will prove useful rather than a bulky object which is useless.

———

الراجل ده حُصّالته ضيقه

This man's crop is narrow.

Said of one with little patience or of one whose means are restricted.

———

نايم في المَيّ وخايف من المطره

He sleeps in the water and he is afraid of the rain.

Said of one who puts a brave face on an almost overwhelming misfortune and yet complains of a trifle.

لو كانت رايحه تمطر كانت غيمت

If it were going to rain, there would be clouds.

« Coming events cast their shadows before ».

اللي يتجوز اثنين يا تاجر يا فاجر

He who marries two is either a merchant or a wanton.

By the word merchant in the East is meant a man of wealth.

مش كل وش يقال له مرحبا

It is not to every face that « Welcome » is said.

Quoted to one who complains of having been coldly received.

يخاف من خياله

He is afraid of his own shadow.

Applied to a timid person.

ما حد يعرف بقدر الميّه الا لما ينشف البير

We never know the worth of water till the well is dry.

مين يتدر يقول البغل في الابريق

Who can affirm that the mule entered the jug ?

This proverb is frequently quoted to show that, though one may conscientiously believe in a thing which may seem extravagant in itself, it is better not to repeat it from fear of being disbelieved. It arises from the following arabic legend.

An Arab who denied the existence of genii bought a mule and took it home. When performing his evening ablutions, he saw the mule enter a jug, and this so scared him, that he ran shouting to the neighbours and told them what he had seen ; they, thinking him mad, endeavoured to appease him, but all in vain ; he vociferated more and more, so that the authorities sent him to the madhouse. When the doctor came to see him, he repeated the account of what he had seen ; whereupon the doctor ordered him to be detained. He continued, upon each visit of the doctor, to repeat his statement until his friends succeeded in persuading him that, if he wished to regain his freedom, he must recant : this he did and the doctor set him at liberty to the great joy of his family and friends. On making his ablutious as before, he again saw the mule this time peeping out of the jug, but on this occasion he contented himself with remarking to the mule : — « Oh yes — I see you well enough, but who would believe me ? and I have had enough of the mad-house ». Needless to say that the genii, to avenge themselves for his disbelief in them, had transformed one of themselves into a mule and as such entered the jug.

What has been may be.

جبال الكحل تفنيها المراود وكثر المال تفنيه السنين

The mountains of « Kohl » will be exhausted by
the Kohl-sticks and the treasures of gold in time.

Quoted to one who spends without forethought.

———

خزين الصيف ينفع للشتاء

The provision of the summer will serve for the
winter.

« *Lay by, like ants, a little store*
For summer lasts not evermore ».

———

من افتكرني ما احتقرني

He who remembers me, does not despise me.

Quoted by one who, having received a small attention,
desires to testify his appreciation.

———

اليوم اللي يفوت ما يجيش زيّه

Another day, like that which is passing, will not
come again.

« *Make hay while the sun shines* ».

Quoted on a festive occasion, as a recommendation to
make the most of it.

شعرَه من ذَقن الخنزير فايده

A bristle from the hog's beard is a gain.

Meaning that a trifle from a miser is to be looked upon as
a gain.

ان رايت أعور عَبر اقلب حجر

When you see a one-eyed man pass, turn up a
stone.

The Egyptian is superstitious and is careful to avoid the
influence of the evil eye and adopts various measures to this
end, amongst others that of turning a stone upon meeting a
one-eyed person, especially early in the morning. Also said
by one friend to another who has not been perceived by an
obnoxious person seeking him, to remind him of his lucky
escape !

قرد يسليني ولا غزال يغمني

A monkey that amuses me rather than a gazelle
that saddens me.

Used to express that amiability in a wife is preferable to
beauty.

مُش كل اللي يُعرَف يقال

It is not all that is known which is to be said.

Quoted to one who has betrayed a confidence.

اللي ياكل العسل يصبر لقرص النحل

He who eats honey must expect the sting of the bees.

You must be prepared to take the consequences of your acts.

قالوا للغراب تسرق الصابون ليه قال الاذيّه طبعي

They said to the crow: Why do you steal soap? He said: doing evil is my nature

Applied to one who continually does harm without any advantage to himself.

عوره وعارجه وكمانها خارجه

One-eyed (woman), lame and out at elbows.

Said of one with every vice and not one redeeming quality.

لما يشبع الحمار يبعزق عليقه

When the donkey has eaten his fill he scatters his fodder.

Applied to one who, from a state of poverty, has become rich and squanders his fortune.

زي التربه ما تردّش ميّت

Like the tomb; it does not give back the dead.
Referring to a bad debtor.

ايش عرّف الحمير في اكل الجنزبيل

What do donkeys know of preserved ginger.
« *Do not cast pearls before swine* ».

ما يسواش ملو ودنه نخاله

He is not worth his ears full of bran.
« *Not worth his salt* ».

اللي يخاف من العفريت يطلع له

Who fears the devil, the devil will appear to him.

Quoted to one who has taken every precaution against an
impending evil and thereby expects to escape it.

فُقَرا ويمشوا مثي الأُمرا

Paupers, yet they walk like grandees.

كتر السلام يقل المعرفه

Many salutations lessen acquaintainship.

Repetition of salutations is common in the East and **the**
above is quoted by one seeking a truce to them.

اذا كان اثنين يقولوا لك راسك مش على اكتافك حسّس عليها

If two tell you your head is not on your shoul-
ders feel for it.

Do not hastily contradict an assertion however **extra-**
vagant it may seem.

لما انت كدا البصل تهلل له السكر ايش تعمل له

If you thus laud the onion, what will you **do**
when you see the sugar.

Said to one who makes a fuss about a small matter. **Sugar**
was scarce and dear, while onions in Egypt have always **been**
plentiful and cheap.

اللي يزمر ما يغطيش ذقنه

Who plays upon the flute does not cover **his**
beard.

Quoted to show that a man committing evil is **no**
more able to conceal his act than a man playing upon **the**
flute is able to cover his beard.

قال يابا علمني الادب قال الكبير ابوك والصغير ابنك واللي قدّك اخوك

Oh my father! teach me manners. He said: (treat)
your elder as your father, your junior as your son
and your equal as your brother.

———

ان غاب القط العب يا فار

If the cat absent himself, play oh mouse.

« *When the cat's away, the mice will play* ».

———

يسكت سنه وينطق بكفر

He keeps silent for a year and (then) utters a
blasphemy.

Applied to one dogged in his silence, only opening his
mouth to utter an absurdity.

———

قبل ما تفصّل قيس

Before cutting the cloth, take the measure.
Before entering upon any business count the cost.

———

جهنم ما فيهاش مراوح

In hell there are no fans.

غوله عملت عزومه قالوا ان شاء الله يكفيها ويكفي عيالها

An ogress gave a feast. They said: It is to be hoped there was enough for herself and her children.

Quoted to one notoriously parsimonious who makes a hollow promise to help another out of a difficulty.

———

ساعه لقلبك وساعه لربك

An hour for your heart and an hour for your God.

« *All work and no play makes Jack a dull boy* ».

———

فار ما طال العسل قال دا مُرّ

The rat could not reach the honey and said it was bitter.

The fox in the Fable, when he could not reach the grapes, said they were sour.

———

اللي عنده مال مُيّره يشتري حمام ويطيّره

He whose wealth perplexes him may buy pigeons and let them fly.

Meaning that there are many ways of scattering money.

انت ابن سبعه

Are you a seven months child ?

Said to a man always in such a hurry that one would think he could not even have waited the usual time to be born.

يعدّ بالالف وينام على البرش

He counts by thousands and sleeps on a mat.

Said of one who, though employed in looking after the riches of another, is himself poor.

بيني وبينه ما صنع الحداد

Between me and him is what the black-smith made.

Quoted to signify that he is on the worst of terms with such a one.

ان حضر العيش يبقى المش شبرقه

When there is bread, curds and whey are an extravagance.

Quoted to one in poor circumstances to reconcile him to his lot.

قلت لك قمّره مش احرقه

I told you to roast not to burn it.

Quoted to inculcate moderation.

من علمني حرف صرت له عبد

Who teaches me one letter I will be his slave.

طاب والا اثنين عور

Cured or both blind ?

This proverb is constantly used and the story of its origin is that a man having a son who had entirely lost the sight of one eye and had the other affected, sent him under the care of his mother to the oculist, and on their return, he anxiously enquired : Is he cured or are both eyes blind ? and is often said to one returning from a commission, who, if he has succeeded, replies « Cured » but if on the contrary he has failed he replies « Both blind ».

ربنا يكره ثلاثة الفقير المتكبر والغني البخيل والعجوز الجاهل

God abhors three : the proud pauper, the rich miser and the ignorant old man.

اِدّيني رغيف ويكِن نظيف

Give me a loaf of bread and let it be clean.

Said of a man who begs and imposes conditions, although
◄ Beggars should not be choosers ».

———

يسرق الكُحل من العين

He steals *kohl* from the eye.

Said of a marvellously dexterous person.

———

بعد ما شاب ودّوه الكتّاب

When he had grown old they sent him to school.

« *What tutor shall we find for a child of sixty*
years old ? ».

———

ان كبر ابنك خاويه

Treat your grown-up son as a brother.

———

تكون جمره تبقى رماد

A gleed will come to ashes.
« *Hot love is soon cold* ».

العصفور بنغماته والمرء بكلامه

A bird by its note and a man by his talk.

———

العطشان يحلم انه في بحر والجيعان في سوق عيش

The thirsty dreams of being in a river and the hungry in the bread-market.

———

ألهي الكلب بعضمه

Distract a dog with a bone.

Used in several ways : Thieves who have been observed should give the observer something to silence him ; to one demanding a loan, give him a small sum and let him go.

———

ما يدخل الدرهم الزغل الا على الصرّاف الشاطر

False coin is passed upon none but the shrewd money-changer.

Used to show that the most shrewd, by over confidence, may be taken in.

———

عصفور في اليد ولا عشره على الشجره

A bird in the hand and not ten on a tree.

زي شرّابة الخرج

Like the tassel of a saddle-bag.

Said of a man absolutely of no utility or influence in a matter. The saddle-bags in the East are generally made of a piece of carpet with a fringe of worsted tassels.

———

من ترك شيء عاش بلاه

Who abandons a thing may live without it.

———

احنا في التفكير وربنا في التدبير

Man proposes and God disposes.

———

غلا وسوء كيل

Dearness yet false measure.

Said to a merchant who charges exorbitantly and at the same time endeavours to cheat.

———

قال عدوَك يحبّك قال يبقى جَنْ

He said: your enemy loves you. The other replied : he has gone mad then.

Indicating his sense of the implacability of his enemy.

صاحب البيت أخبر بما فيه

The owner (or the master) of the house best knows what it contains.

« *A fool knows more in his own house than a wise man in another's* ».

———

هو يعوم زي الرصاص

He swims like lead.

———

اعلّمك السرقه تحط ايدك في جيبي

I taught you to steal and you thrust your hand in my pocket.

Said to one who returns evil for good.

———

الأيد اللي تُمد ولا تضرب بش تستاهل قطعها

The hand that threatens without striking deserves to be cut off.

———

زي اولاد الحاره زمّاره تلمهم وكفّ يبعزقهم

Like the street-children, a sound of music collects them and a blow disperses them.

Said of those easily distracted from their work.

خلّاه على الازض السوداء

He left him on the black ground.

Said of one who has deprived another of all his means leaving him absolutely penniless.

ان ضربت إوْجع وان اطعمت إشبع

When you strike, hurt; when you feed (a man) satiate him.

Do nothing by halves.

اللي على راسه بَطحه يحسّس عليها

He who has a wound on the head will touch it.

Implying that a man who has committed an offence is sure, however inadvertently, to call attention to it, and the proverb is quoted generally by one who is charged with an offence of which he is innocent.

اللي واكل لحمه نَيّة توجعه بطنه

Whoever has eaten raw meat will have a stomach ache.

Applied as the preceding proverb.

14

مصر خيرها لغيرها

The riches of Egypt are for others.

Quoted by Egyptians when they see the capital and enterprise of Europeans prospering.

———

عاوز قط خشب يصطاد ولا ياكلش

He wants a wooden cat that catches mice and
does not eat.

Applied to one who is exacting and grudges payment.

———

مين يعرف عيشه في سوق الغزل

Who can recognise « Eyshah » in the market of
the cotton-yarn ?

Quoted to show that where you are unknown, an unwon-
ted licence will not be remarked.

———

ما قدرش على الحمار اتشطّر على البردعه

He could not get the better of the donkey and he
turned against the saddle.

Quoted to a vituperative man who, having met with
more than his equal in vituperation, turns upon a diffident
man.

اكثرُ المعزِّبين شوامت

Most condolers are revengers.

Said by one to an old enemy who comes to sympathise with him in his misfortune.

———

ما يضايق الزريبه الا النعجه الغريبه

Nothing disturbs the sheep-fold like a strange sheep.

Quoted by a bride on finding herself coldly received by her husband's family : Also by one who on taking up a new post perceives that his colleagues look askance at him.

———

شخشخ يلتمّوا عليك

Jingle (your coins) and they (people) will gather.

Said to a niggardly fellow complaining of want of company.

———

ماشي ندّك وامشي على قدّك وكل عيش اللي يحبّك وادخل بيت اللي يستغناك

Frequent those of your age, spend according to your means, eat the bread of him who loves you and enter the house of him who regards you.

الإيد الغريبة تخرب البيوت العامره

The hand of the stranger ruins flourishing houses.

Said to one who has married his daughter to a stranger who turns out to be a spend-thrift, instead of having married her to a near connection or relative, as is customary in the East.

———

زي المنشار ياكل طالع نازل

Like the pit-saw that eats up and down.

Applied to one notoriously addicted to taking bribes.

———

ان حبّك الريس امسح ايدك في القلع

If the captain likes you, you may wipe your hands on the sail.

If one is well with his chief, his shortcomings will be overlooked.

———

النجوم في السماء اقرب لك

The stars in heaven are nearer to you.

Quoted to one engaged in a wild scheme to indicate the impossibility of a favourable issue.

خاص السلام بقي تفتيش الاكمام

The salutations are over and the searching in the sleeves has begun.

The sleeves of an Arab's garment are both wide and long and thus afford easy concealment ; the above is quoted by one who has been ostensibly invited out of politeness and who finds himself cross-examined by his host in order to extract information upon a certain subject. It is commonly quoted by any one persistently questioned.

———

الوقوع في البلا ولا انتظاره

Misfortune itself rather than suspense.

———

الخوف يرجّ الجوف

Fear makes the body tremble.

———

اسأل عن الجار قبل الدار

Ask about the neighbour before (taking) the house.

———

خذ الرفيق قبل الطريق

Choose the companion before (commencing) the journey.

اللي يعمل به القرد يعلّق به الحمار

What is gained by the monkey only serves for the donkey.

A popular show in Cairo is that of a performing monkey and a very small donkey. The showman makes the above remark to show that he has gained no more than his expenses. The proverb is quoted by any one whose gains barely suffice to keep his family.

———

زي الغجر لا يوحشهم من غاب ولا يؤانسهم من حضر

Like the gypsies : with no care for the absent and indifference for those present.

Generally applied to one devoid of family affection.

———

الاصطبل ضيّق والحمار رفّاص

The stable is narrow and the donkey is restive.

Said to one of a company in a small room who by awkward movements causes inconvenience.

———

الحيطه اللي لها سنّاد ما تقعش

The wall that has a support does not fall.

Said to encourage a man who fears that he may lose his post, but who is befriended by a man of influence.

في افراحهم منسيّه وفي حزنهم مدعيه

At their rejoicings I am forgotten and to their mourning I am invited.

Said by Arab women, of one who is more free with her invitations when services are to be rendered, as at a funeral, than when guests have to be entertained, as at a wedding.

الميّه تكذّب الغطّاس

The water gives the lie to the (pretended) diver.

Quoted by one whose prowess is questioned and who is desirous of being put to the test.

علّمناه على الشحاته سبقنا على الابواب

We taught him begging and he had the start of us at the doors.

Said of one whom you have informed of your intentions and who forestalls you.

مصائب قوم عند قوم فوائد

The misfortunes of some are advantages to others.

« *It's an ill wind that blows nobody any good* ».

قال السمك يطلّع نار قال كانت الميه تطفيه

He said : the fish throw out fire. He replied : the
water would have extinguished it.

Quoted to one making a highly improbable statement.

دا وشّك ولّا ضو القمر

Is it your face or the moonshine ?

Said by one friend to another paying a visit after a pro-
longed absence. In English. « You are quite a stranger ».

افتكرنا القط جانا ينط

We thought of the cat and it came leaping.
« *Talk of the devil and he is sure to appear* ».

أعمى وعايز يعمل صرّاف

He is blind and would be a money-changer.

Said of a man who seeks a post for which he is mani-
festly unfit.

الغرقان يتلهف على قشّايه

The drowning man sighs for a straw.

ثلاث اشياء يذّلوا الانسان المرا ولو كانت مرهم والدين ولو كان درهم
والسؤال ولو اين الطريق

Three things will make a man feel subdued : A
woman if she were a balm. A debt of even a drachm.
A question, even if it be only to know the road.

———

الناي في كمّي والريح في فمّي

The flute is in my sleeve and the breath in my
mouth.

Often quoted among friends to express : « I am ready »,
« at your service ».

———

حصيرة الصيف واسعة

The mat of summer is wide.

It is customary in summer in Egypt for the villagers
to sleep outside their huts for coolness, hence the sleeping mat
or open space is wide.

———

خِفّها تعوم

Make it light and it will float.

Said to a man to induce him to pay at least part of his
debt in order to avoid trouble befalling him.

ان فاتك الميري اتمرَّغ في ترابه

If Government gets rid of you, roll yourself in its dust.

The desire to be in Government service is universal in Egypt : a man in easy circumstances will work for a nominal pay for this coveted privilege ; another will refuse a lucrative post in a private establishment for a pittance in the Government service.

The following story is current in illustration of this. A merchant brought two fine donkeys from Arabia and sold them in the market. One was bought by a rich merchant and the other for the Scavenging Dept. of the Government. The merchant's donkey was led to the river, soaped and scrubbed every morning ; was fed with a liberal allowance of beans ; had a handsome blue cloth saddle, embroidered reins, silver nose and curb chains ; was lightly worked, having nothing to do but carry the merchant from his house to business in the morning and back in the evening. The other donkey had a very different lot, being harnessed to a dust cart, dirty, ill fed, overworked and beaten. One day the two met and, recognizing each other, the merchant's donkey remarked upon his old friend's dirty condition. Yes, replied he, but I am in Government service. At this moment the driver vociferated and beat him to make him drag the heavy cart which he could hardly move, and, upon his friend's condoling with him, replied as before « Yes, but I am in the Government service ».

―――――

رزقه بين رجليه

His luck (lies) between his legs.

Said of one who invariably succeeds in his undertakings.

اللي تكرهه انت يحبّه غيرك

What you dislike another may like.

Quoted to one who affects to despise an offer.

———

النّاس على دين ملوكهم

The people are of the religion of their kings.

« *Like priest like people* ».

———

كل جديد وله لذّه

Everything new has its pleasure.

« *Novelty gives pleasure* ».

———

فوت على عدوّك جيعان ولا تفوتش عليهِ عريان

Pass by your enemy hungry but do not pass him naked.

Keep up a good appearance under difficulties.

———

أنجس من فارة الحبس

More cunning than a prison rat.

دا في المشمس

That is for the apricots.

The above is most frequently quoted and is employed
jokingly in reply to a request too preposterous to be granted :
somewhat as « Don't you wish you may get it ? » is used.

It originated from the association of two fruit sellers, an
Egyptian and a Syrian, who took it by turns to hold the scale,
and to fill it. The Egyptian held the scale during the
apricot season and, whilst he was occupied weighing, he observed his partner, the Syrian, frequently eating the ripest
apricots. When the grape season came, the Egyptian, while
his partner was engaged in weighing, ate the grapes by the
bunch ; the Syrian remonstrated, saying that he should take
them one by one ; upon which the Egyptian replied : Da fil
meshmesh : or « That is for (or applies to) the apricots.

من قلة الخيل شدّوا على الكلاب

From lack of horses they saddled the dogs.
For want of people of worth the unworthy were taken.

قالوا للكلاب دي رايحه تمطر فطاير قالوا كانت ندّعت جرايه

They said to the dogs : It is going to rain cakes.
They replied : (If so) it would have drizzled barley-
bread.

There is generally some indication of what is going to
happen.

ما يعرف عدوّه من حبيبه

He does not know his enemy from his friend.

Meaning that such an one's intelligence is not of a **high** order.

———

جوزي ما حكني دار عشيقي ورايا بنبوت

My husband has not controlled me, yet my lover runs after me with a club.

Said to an interfering person.

———

التاجر لما يفتقر يدوّر في الدفاتر القُدُم

When a merchant becomes poor, he will rummage amongst his old books.

In the hope of finding an overlooked debtor.

———

لا ظلام كالجهل

No darkness like ignorance.

———

الانسان يستغني عن اصحابه وليس عن جيرانه

Man can do without his friends, but not without his neighbours.

شعيرنا ولا قمح غيرنا

Our own barley and not the wheat of another.

Meaning it is preferable to eat the frugal meal prepared at home to eating that of another however sumptuous it may be.

———

لا تأمن لمرَه اذا صلّت ولا للشمس اذا ولّت

Do not trust a woman if she prays, nor the sun when it is clouded.

Meaning that the semblance of sanctity may cloak vice as clouds over the sun may indicate rain.

———

ان لم تزاحم ما يقع لك شيء في الخُرج

If you do not push forward, nothing will fall in your wallet.

« A closed mouth catcheth no flies ».

———

مال الدست يغلي قال من كثر ناره

Why is the cauldron boiling? He said : from abundance of heat.

Said of a man bubbling over with rage.

زي اللي عُمره ما داق الاكل

(He eats) as though he had never tasted food in his life.

Said of a glutton.

———

الشبعان يِفتّ للجيعان فتّ بطي

The satiated breaks the bread for the hungry too slowly.

Said by one seeking aid and being kept in suspense.

———

اللي معاه القمر ما يبالِيش بالنجوم

He who has the moon cares not for the stars.

Meaning that he who has the chief with him need not care about the subordinates.

———

اللي يعرّف الشحّات بابه يا طول عذابه

He who makes known to the beggar his door lays himself open to lengthy importunities.

Used as a caution against complying with the first request of an impecunious person.

بدن وافر وقلب كافر

A bulky body and an unfaithful heart.

Said of one who receives his prosperity in a thankless spirit.

ان كانت الدنيا لواحد ما تكفهش

If the world belonged to one it would not suffice.

Applied to one whose greed for wealth is insatiable.

الظاهر لنا والخفي على الله

What is manifest is for us ; what is hidden for God.

Said of one whose appearance of innocence may be only the cloak of hypocrisy.

الابريق الردي علاقته ،اكنه

The worst jug has a solid handle.

Implying that the more precious things are liable to be lost while the commoner things remain.

من أحسن لي واساء الى غيري عدّيته من المحسنين

Who does good to me and ill to others, I consider him a benefactor.

« *Speak of a man as you find him* »,

رضيوا الخصمين وامتنع القاضي

The litigants were of accord and the « Cadi » objected.

The « Cadi » or judge is said not always to be immaculate but sometimes to have an eye to self interest.

———

ادخل بشي تبقى إشي يفرشوا لك ويقدّموا لك كل شي

Enter with something and you will be somebody: they will prepare for you the bed and present you with everything.

When seeking hospitality or returning home from a voyage, do not be empty-handed. Also used to recommend a present being given in order to attain your end.

———

اللي يعيش يشوف كثير واللي يمشي يشوف اكثر

Who lives sees, but who travels sees more.

———

البغل العجوز ما يخفش من الجلاجل

The old mule is not scared at the jingling of the bells.

اللي يروح وحده للقاضي يرجع راضي

Who goes by himself to the « Cadi » returns
contented.

Said of one who, having made his plaint alone to one in
authority, returns contented, the suggestion being that, had
his adversary been present, things might have taken another
turn.

بلدنا صغيره ونعرف بعض

Our villlage is small and we all know each other.

Said to one whose mendacity is well known.

ورّاه النجوم في وسط الظهر

He made him see the stars at mid-day.

Meaning that by ill usage he made his life a burden
to him.

زي الحمام يهوى براج براج

Like the pigeons , they fly from one dove-cot to
another.

Said of a man with whims and fancies.

كُثر الحزن يعلّم البكا وكُثر الفرح يعلّم الغُنا

Much sorrow teaches weeping and much joy teaches mirth.

———

اللُقمة الكــبيره ٠تقف في الزور

Too big a mouthful will stick in the throat.

Too great mendacity or peculation will be found out

———

زي الشمعه تنوّر على الناس وتحرق روحها

Like a candle, giving light to others and consuming itself.

Said of one who impoverishes himself in serving others

———

ايش وصّتك حماتك قال اللي ماجا على بالي طيّب وايش وصّتك مراتك قال ايش كانت اشغالي

What did your mother-in-law ask you. He Said: something I should not have imagined. Well! and what did your wife ask for: She asked how was my business.

The wife thought only of her husband's interest, but the mother-in-law sought something quite disproportionate to his means. Quoted to show real friendship.

اللي ياكل مرقة السلطان تنحرق شفّته

Who eats the Sultan's soup will have his lips
burnt.

« *He that eats the king's goose shall be choked
with the feathers* ».

زي الاعمى يغمّض ويسبّ

Like the blind man, he shuts his eyes and re-
viles.

« *An angry man opens his mouth and shuts his
eyes* ». Cato.

ابليس مايخربش بيته

The devil does not destroy his own house.

Applied to a man of ill-gotten wealth, squandering reck-
lessly, implying that he is unlikely to be ruined, for « the devil
will take care of his own ». Or in discussing the probability
of a sick man recovering, the above proverb is often employed

---

دخان بلا قهوه سلطان بلا فروه

Tobacco without coffee is like a prince without
furs·

The « Chibouque » or a cigarette is always presented
with coffee in the East.

مالك ساكت قال ادبّر لكم في داهيه

Why are you so silent. He said: I am medita-
ting a mischief to you.

من خفَّ عقله تعبِت رجليه

A light mind will tire the legs.

Said derisively to one who comes seeking a service
which cannot be rendered.

إِيد واحده ما تزقفش

One hand cannot applaud.

Used to show the need of co-operation.

كل طلعه ولها نزله

Every rise has a fall.

« *Every tide has its ebb* »

برد الصيف أحدّ من السيف

Cold in summer is sharper than a sword.

بدْأل خطوطِك والحمره امسحي عماصِك يا زمره

Instead of blacking your eye-brows and eyelids and painting your cheeks, wipe the rheum (from your eyes), oh hussey.

Said to a woman who neglects personal cleanliness.

بير تشرب منه ما ترميش فيه حجر

In the well from which you drink, throw no stone.

Do not destroy that from which you derive benefit.

ياقنديلين وشمعه يا على الظلام جمعه

Either two lamps and a candle, or darkness for a week.

Said in reproach of reckless extravagance.

الشجره اللي تضلل عليك ما تدعيش بقطعها

Do not pray for the destruction of the tree that shades you.

Do not pray for the destruction of your benefactor.

حرامي بلا بيّنه سلطان زمانه

A thief without witnesses (against him) is the Sultan of his time.

By the Moslem law, a conviction is seldom obtained except upon the production of at least two witnesses.

طلع النهار وبان العوار

The morning broke and defects were apparent.

Said of a disappointing bride. The bridegroom, having only seen his bride by the deceptive light of the chandeliers, is sometimes disappointed at her appearance by day.

الاَكل في الشبعان خساره

To feed a satiated man is waste.

It is idle to bestow alms where there is no need.

واحد شايل دقنه والثاني تعبان فيها

One carries (or wears) his beard and another is tired of it.

Quoted to one who reproaches another for acting as he pleases.

زي الكبريت ما يصدّقش الاّ لما يقرّب للنار

Like matches, he does not believe till he touches
fire.

Said of one so incredulous that he will not believe even
in fire till he has burnt his fingers.

———

زي ابريق الحِمَلي دايمًا يرشّح

Like the water-vessel, always oozing.

Said of a man constantly perspiring.

———

زي الحرّوب قنطار خشب على درهم سكر

Like the fruit of the Carob-tree, a « kantar » of
wood to a « drachm » of sugar.

Applied to one whose mental powers are not developed in
proportion to his bodily physique.

———

النار فاكهة الشتا

The fire is the dessert of the Winter.

Being generally lightly clad, the Egyptian peasants sleep
in winter on the top of the capacious oven to be found in all
their huts, and the upper classes sit round a brazier of glowing
charcoal in the morning and evening.

زيتنا في دقيقنا

Our oil is in our flour.

Said by a relative to induce two relatives to marry.

———

بيت السبع ما يخلاش من العظام

The lion's den is not free from bones.

Quoted to a man who has money to spare, though he denies it.

———

قالوا يا جحا عِدّ غَنَمَك قال واحده راقده وواحده واقفه

They said : Oh Goha ! count your sheep ! He said : One is lying down and one standing up.

Intended to indicate restricted means.

———

ما تعرجش قدّام مكسّحين

Do not limp before cripples.

« *Name not a rope in his house that hanged himself* ».

———

ان ما كانش لك أهل ناسب

If you have no relatives, get married.

قالوا للقرده اتبرقعي قالت دا وش واخذ على الفضيحة

They told the she-monkey to veil her face. She said : I am too brazen.

Applied to one utterly devoid of shame. The use of the veil is almost universal with Mohamedan women and is considered as a token of modesty and self-respect.

مزيّن فتح باقرع استفتح

A barber opened his shop and his first customer was scurfy.

Quoted to signify that the day's work has commenced inauspiciously.

الحيطه الواطيه ينطّوا عليها الكلاب

Over the low wall the dogs will leap.

« All lay the load on the willing horse ».

لما يطيب العليل ينسى جميل المداوي

When the patient is cured he forgets the healing hand.

Said of an ungrateful man.

Arabic language studies and dictionaries from Hippocrene...

ARABIC-ENGLISH DICTIONARY
450 pages • 5 1/2 x 8 1/4 • 15,000 entries
0-7818-0153-2 • W • $14.95pb • (487)

ARABIC-ENGLISH/ENGLISH-ARABIC STANDARD DICTIONARY
900 pages • 5 1/2 x 8 1/2
0-7818-0383-7 • W • $24.95pb • (195)

ARABIC GRAMMAR OF THE WRITTEN LANGUAGE
560 pages • 5 1/2 x 8 1/4
0-87052-101-2 • W • $19.95pb • (397)

MODERN MILITARY DICTIONARY: ENGLISH-ARABIC/ARABIC-ENGLISH
250 pages • 5 1/2 x 8 1/2
0-7818-0243-1 NA • $14.95pb • (214)

SAUDI ARABIC BASIC COURSE: URBAN HAJAZI DIALECT
288 pages • 6 1/2 x 8 1/2 • 50 lessons index glossary
0-7818-0257-1 • W • $14.95pb • (171)

ARABIC FOR BEGINNERS
186 pages • 5 1/4 x 8 1/4
0-7818-0114-1 NA • $9.95pb • (18)

LET US CONVERSE IN ARABIC
156 pages • 5 1/2 x 8 1/2
0-7818-0562-7 • $11.95pb • NA • (702)

MASTERING ARABIC
320 pages • 5 1/4 x 8 1/4
0-87052-922-6 USA • $14.95pb • (501)
<u>**2 Cassettes:**</u> **0-87052-984-6 • USA • $12.95 • (507)**

ARABIC HANDY DICTIONARY
120 pages • 5 x 7 3/4
0-87052-960-9 • USA • $8.95pb • (463)

TREASURY OF ARABIC LOVE POEMS, QUOTATIONS & PROVERBS
in Arabic (Romanized) and English
edited by Farid Bitar
128 pages • 5 x 7
0-7818-0395-0 • W • $11.95 • (71)

All prices subject to change. To order Hippocrene Books, contact your local bookstore, call (718) 454-2366, or write to: HIPPOCRENE BOOKS, 171 Madison Avenue, New York, NY 10016. Please enclose check or money order, adding $5.00 shipping (UPS) for the first book and $.50 for each additional book.